Camping: A 1 Guide to Starting Camping

Camping Gear, Where to Stay, Outdoor Recipes, Survival

by Mark Stone

Table of Contents

Disclaimer

While all attempts have been made to verify the information provided in this book, the author does not assume any responsibility for errors, omissions, or contrary interpretations of the subject matter contained within. The information provided in this book is for educational and entertainment purposes only. The reader is responsible for his or her own actions and the author does not accept any responsibilities for any liabilities or damages, real or perceived, resulting from the use of this information.

Introduction

So, you have decided you want to go camping. Excellent! Whether you are doing so to connect with nature, get away from the fast-paced life of the modern world, or recover childhood memories, camping can be a wonderful experience.

For many of us, our childhood memories include camping with our parents. At least once in the summer, Mom and Dad would pack up the fishing poles, sleeping bags and cooler full of food to go spend a week hiking through the woods, swimming in a cool lake and huddling around the campfire at night roasting hot dogs and marshmallows.

And for most of us those are fond memories indeed, memories we hope to give our own children one day.

Of course, maybe you do not have a family but still want to get back in touch with nature and rekindle some of those early childhood memories.

In either case, if you haven't been out roughing it since you were a child or if you have never been camping at all, it can easily turn into an unpleasant experience that you won't want to repeat if you jump in without knowing what you are doing.

That's where this guide comes in. Certainly, we won't be covering every aspect of every kind of camping that you could possibly do in this short book.

Our purpose here is simply to give you some basic tips and point you in the right direction so that no matter where you are and what sort of camping you are wanting to try you will be able to go into it prepared.

And being prepared, you and whoever you are camping with will want to get out again and again. And while the main focus of this guide is family camping, any beginner should be able to benefit as many of the considerations involved and gear needed will be similar.

We will be spending time looking at the different kinds of camping there are, how to find different camp sites, what kind of gear to bring, what sort of food you should plan on and how to prepare for emergencies like a sprained ankle on the trail, or getting rained in with a bunch of bored kids.

So, let's grab a pair of comfortable shoes, pick up a walking stick and get started.

Chapter 1 – Where should you camp?

Alright, it's time to get the kids loaded up in the minivan so they can experience the outdoors the way you remember it. But there are some things to consider first.

How comfortable is everyone with stepping away from the comforts of daily life? How plugged in are you? Have your children gone swimming anywhere besides a pool before? In short, do you live in the big city or the suburbs and how much of a shock is the camping experience going to be?

When you have that figured out, you can decide between three basic options:

- Resort camping – This is arguably not even camping as you will be in a cabin or a high end camper on a concrete pad with electricity and very likely running water. However, this option could prove exactly what you need to ease the family into the idea of camping.

  Resorts also will often have a pool, a playground, convenience store, Wi-Fi, and organized activities for the kids.

  A resort will also still be rural enough that you can get out and find some good trails to hike and places to ride horses and other such activities, though there may be more people around than you would like.

- Modern camping – This is very similar to resort camping in that the site may well have water and electric hookups. Even barring the water hookups at the individual campsite, there will be bathroom facilities with running water on site.

The difference chiefly lies in that the extras like organized activities, pools and internet will not be available. Such places also tend to be located in more rural areas with many of the same outdoor options (horseback riding, hiking, kayaking) available and in somewhat less demand.

- Rustic camping – Often, a typical campground will have modern sections with electricity available and other sections that are designated as rustic. These will be little more than a cleared-off section of forest with perhaps a raised platform for your tent and a fire pit.

  This is for the family that wants to dive into camping for the first time and is not deterred by the lack of heat and electricity or by the kinds of insects that tend to populate the forest.

  Bathroom facilities are also minimal and are likely nothing more than an old-fashioned pit toilet. These kinds of campsites are also often in protected areas that require you to carry your gear to the site rather than driving right up and parking right next to your tent.

  On the plus side, the grounds are likely to be quiet with ample opportunity for spotting wildlife during the day and stargazing at night.

Beyond the campsite

Now that you have decided what sort of camping you want to do, it is time to decide where to go.

The internet, as in most things, is an invaluable resource here. Sites like CampingCanada.com have a comprehensive list not only of campgrounds, but of the services available.

You can find rustic sites, sites with full electric and water hookups and campgrounds with on-site laundry. Whatever your particular requirements, websites like CampingCanada will help you find the place that meets them.

Once you have narrowed your options down to a small handful of appealing campgrounds, you should begin searching for local attractions. These will help break up the trip and provide some educational opportunities as well.

Some things you might look for are:

- **Kayak/canoe rental**

- **Bike rental**

- **Beaches**

- **Fishing**

- **Local wildlife**

- **Hiking trails**

Another thing to keep in mind is exposing the family to any local culture. Look for campgrounds in places where a festival might be taking place, or local museums that can help educate the family about the region's original inhabitants, any connections to events like the War of 1812, the European settling of Canada and if you are on the east coast, any sites connected to the early Viking settlements in the country.

Be creative. Most areas have some interesting history or character that is unique and you would never learn about otherwise.

There are other considerations but we will save those for the section in which we'll discuss how to prepare for the unexpected.

When to camp

Now, it may seem obvious that one should camp in the summer but there is actually far more to consider than merely whether or not it is snowing.

One thing to avoid is trying to camp during any major holidays. Parks fill up quickly and even if you can manage to get into a campground, it will be full of people generously and loudly celebrating with the aid of plenty of alcohol.

And that can certainly get in the way of getting the children to sleep and being able to enjoy the rest of the trip.

Many parks will allow you to view available campsites and make reservations online, allowing you to pick a time, or area of the grounds that is less crowded. Keep in mind that this may also mean being far away from the services you chose the campground for.

Weather is also an important consideration. Clearly, no one can predict whether it will rain or not in a given area two months in advance. But you can research what sort of weather is normal for wherever it is you choose to camp.

Naturally, you will want to avoid rain. But also try to avoid the times of year that are most prone to heat and humidity. There are several reasons for this.

One is the obvious discomfort that comes from those conditions, especially if you are camping in a tent with small children.

Another is the fact that those conditions are very favorable for insects, especially the most notorious of pests, the mosquito.

If you avoid the wet season too much, this might an effect on the scenery as rivers and waterfalls that are largely fed by the melting of the winter snowfall may diminish or disappear completely.

Finally, if you pick the height of the hot and dry period there may be restrictions on any open flame in order to prevent forest fires.

And camping isn't camping without a fire at night. As a general rule, focus on late spring or early summer to get the best combination of scenery, crowds and weather.

Chapter 2 – What to bring. Essentials and beyond.

Now that you have decided where and when you are going to camp, it is time to look at what sort of gear to bring. My first piece of advice is to rent or borrow from friends and family before buying.

The fact is that camping gear is expensive and takes up a lot of space. More than one family has spent a thousand dollars or more on camping gear only to find it collecting dust in the attic a year or two later.

Rent-A-Tent Canada and Canadian Adventure Rentals offer rentals of all the equipment you will need, including prearranged packages so all you have to do is order the package you want and enjoy the great outdoors.

If you cannot access a rental service, or borrow from anyone, or have simply decided that you are going to buy because you are determined that yours will be a camping family, then we need to go over some of the basic gear you will need.

We are going to focus on tent camping in this section, since if you are using a camper or RV of some sort you will mostly just be bringing food and things for the trail, which will be the same weather or not you are in a tent or a camper.

There is quite a bit to think about here as you are likely starting from scratch. First, let's just look at a list of the gear needed and other, optional equipment.

Essentials:

- **Tent** – The biggest consideration is the size of the tent needed. And the biggest rule here is that the packaging lies. If you need a four person tent, buy a five or six person tent.

  Whoever decides how many people can sleep in a given tent must be very small and assume that no one will be putting their clothes or other gear in with them.

  Also, be sure to spend enough money that you get a tent that is sturdy enough to not rip while you are setting it up, won't leak if it does happen to rain a bit and is simple to assemble.

  There are not many worse ways to start a camping trip that fighting with a bunch of rickety poles and flimsy fabric while the family waits impatiently. To make sure you get something worth your time and money, make sure you read any customer reviews and practice setting up the tent in your yard before the trip.

  Stove/grill – Naturally, you need to eat while you are camping. You may well have visions of cooking everything over an open flame. Don't count on it.

  The wood available may be expensive, or of poor quality and not burn well, or long enough.

  The simplest option is to go with a common camping stove/grill powered by propane. The propane canisters are small and relatively low cost. It is also easy to start and keep the flame going.

  The stoves are also versatile enough to allow you to cook everything from pancakes to burgers. Make sure you bring appropriate cookware. Stainless steel or iron give the best results and will stand up to repeated uses better.

- **Roasting sticks** – There is not much to think about here. These are simply metal poles with prongs on the end generally used for the roasting of hot dogs and marshmallows over an open flame.

  Make sure that the poles are long enough so you don't have to hover over the fire and have wood or heavy-duty rubber handles so the heat doesn't conduct down the pole and become uncomfortable to hold.

- **Pie irons** – Another fine staple of camping trips is what is sometimes called the "hobo pie." These are made from two heavily buttered slices of bread placed in iron squares that clamp together and can then be placed directly in the fire to cook.

  You can place nearly anything between the bread, including cheese and pie fillings. The result is a tasty and easy treat that anyone can make and will be sure to help create exactly the kind of memories you are looking for.

- **Flashlights** – You probably already have flashlights around the home. Make sure that they are durable, bright and have fresh batteries. If you need to by new lights, don't buy the cheapest thing you find in the store.

  They will likely fall apart, not be very bright or drain your battery far too quickly. Plan on spending a minimum of ten dollars each so you get something that will last longer than one trip.

- **Lantern** – A lantern is essential primarily for rainy nights where you and the family are huddled in the tent reading stories or playing games together.

  They can be set up without tipping over with less difficulty than a flashlight and easily illuminate the entire tent. Get an LED lantern as they are far quieter than a propane powered one and do not produce any dangerous fumes.

- **Bug repellent** – Even the best planned trip will run into bugs. Mosquitos are the most obvious to protect against but depending on the area and the time of year, ticks and biting flies should also be a consideration.

  Check the packaging for a list of the insects they protect against and the warnings before application.

- **Cooler** – This is another place where you don't want to buy the cheapest thing available. You don't have to get the top of the line either. Check the packaging to see how long it claims to keep food cold for and then check customer reviews to see if those claims hold up.

  Other essential things to look for in a cooler is a drain spout so you can drain it as the ice melts and wheels and an extending handle to make it easy to transport.

- **Sleeping bags** – If you are camping with young children, you really do not need to spend a lot of money here. There is no need to spend a hundred or more dollars on a subzero mummy bag if you are camping in the summer with a five-year old.

Simply check to be sure that the sleeping bags for you and your children are large enough for you and the kids and that they will keep you warm if the temperature lowers a few degrees at night.

- **Pocket knife** – It is difficult to predict exactly where you will need a pocket knife on your trip; cutting a rope, whittling a stick for an extra roaster or prying an interesting rock out of the ground.

  Spending somewhere between $10-30 should be sufficient for your needs. Make sure that there is some kind of locking device so the blade will not fold back on you while using it.

- **First aid kit** – Make sure that whatever kit you buy has more than simply Band-Aids. Look at different options, picking one with different sizes of Band-Aids, gauze or bandages, hospital tape, aspirin and alcohol wipes for cleaning any wounds.

- **Camping chairs** – This is another item you should not be looking to spend a lot of money on. For the kids, you can get almost any simple folding chair.

  For the adults, look for something with arms and cup holders. You will quickly find yourself getting tired of reaching down to the ground for everything if you don't.

- **Fire starters** – Naturally, you will want a fire so that you can actually roast those marshmallows and hot dogs. Getting it started can be more difficult than you think though.

And as easy as it sounds to get small, dry twigs and leaves and build up to a proper log, just getting the twigs started can take more than a simple match if it has been wet or you are inexperienced with starting a fire.

Fortunately, there are plenty of options out there. One of the simplest are small, white fuel pellets that are often sold in the camping section of your local department store.

They are marketed as a survival fuel but they burn so hot and fast that they are more useful as a fire starter.

You will still need a match to light them but they start very easily.

Optional:

- **Multitool** – This is almost an essential item as it has so many potential uses that you are almost certain to use it at least once. The original multitool is the classic Swiss Army Knife.

  With at least one knife blade, a straight and a Phillips screwdriver (and countless other options) the Swiss Army Knife became a standard pack item for many people.

  They have been supplanted in recent years by the advent of tools that are built around a simple pliers. Plan on spending at least $30 as cheaper models are cheaper for a reason.

  Look for either a Gerber or Leatherman as these are common and represent the best of the affordable multitools on the market. A good multitool can also take the place of the above mentioned pocket knife.

- **Compass** – A compass is primarily useful if you are going hiking in the deep woods, far from any marked trails. This is not recommended for first-time campers! It is still wise to bring one along so that you can get familiar with their use.

  It is more complicated that simply finding north. Another way to use a compass is to get your bearings at night for stargazing purposes.

- **Star chart** – Again, useful for stargazing if you have clear nights. You can also find many apps in the Google Play Store or iOS App Store to help you identify the constellations as well as significant stars and planets visible wherever you happen to be.

  Most apps will also contain images and information about various astronomical objects.

- **Binoculars** – Find a good pair of binoculars to take with you. You can use them at night to resolve features of the moon more clearly than with your eye or turn them to the Milky Way for amazing starscapes.

  During the day, use them for wildlife spotting on the trail. Again, plan on spending a fair amount of money as you are looking for a good mix of durability, portability and magnification.

- **Trail maps** – Research the available trails in the area you are camping and get maps that will usually be available in the campground/park offices.

This will help you find trails that are at a difficulty level appropriate for your family and also have some impressive scenery for everyone to enjoy.

- **Backpack** – If this is your first outing with children, chances are that you are not going to be going out hiking for more than a couple hours at a time. So if you already have a fairly sturdy pack with enough storage for binoculars, a first aid kit, water and trail snacks, you should be fine.

  If not, I would still not spend a lot of money yet. Make $60 your limit and look for something with plenty of pockets, quality zippers and loops to be able to hang extra equipment from.

  Another feature that will be nice to have if you get more into hiking is a storage area for a hydration bladder. These are basically thick bags that can hold a liter of water and come equipped with a straw.

  A pack that can accommodate one will also have hole to run the straw through so it will always be available when you are thirsty.

- **Wildlife / plant guides** – If you have not been outdoors much, it is very likely that you will not be able to identify or discuss the many beautiful plants and animals that you might encounter on the trail.

  Buy a physical guide appropriate to your region that is loaded with colorful pictures to help you identify what is all around. These guides will also be full of useful information about what plants are poisonous and which are edible.

- **Hiking boots** – Much like with the backpack, whatever comfortable footwear you already have will be more than sufficient for your needs.

  If you want to plan for the future though, plan on spending a bare minimum of $50 as boots will be one of the most important purchases you make.

  Do not buy them online unless absolutely necessary. Do your research and read the reviews online but when it comes time to buy, find a local shoe or sports store and spend time talking with a sales rep and trying on different options.

  You will spend more money but save your feet a lot of pain in the bargain.

- **Fishing equipment** – One of the things that many people enjoy about spending time outdoors is fishing, a time-honored bonding tradition between fathers and their children since someone first put a hook on a string.

  If you haven't been in a long time, spend some time learning what kind of fish you can expect to find in the streams and ponds you will be near and what sort of bait to use.

  Don't get too elaborate just yet, focus on one or two kinds of fish that don't need a lot of equipment. And for bait, you may be able to use worms you get out of the dirt anyway.

  The one place you may want to spend some money is the reel itself. You want something that will cast smoothly and not bind up on you.

Chapter 3 – What are we going to eat?

Eating is one of the most important aspects of camping. Big breakfasts, relaxing dinners, great treats like s'mores and pies are some of the things that every kid loves about getting outside of the house for a few days.

The key here is to keep it simple. Whether it is breakfast, lunch, dinner, or snacks, it is best to focus on food that is high in protein and easy to make with a minimum of equipment.

Also, you can either bring camping dishes and cutlery along or purchase paper plates and cups so you don't have to wash. If you choose the latter, make sure to bring along enough trash bags to properly dispose of your trash.

Now let's take a quick look at what you might make for every meal of the day.

Breakfast

You can largely plan anything that you would normally make at home. Cereal of course is very simple as all you need is a bowl and spoon.

But your propane powered stove is more than capable of making bacon, eggs and pancakes, giving you enough options to spend a week away from home.

A quick tip about the pancakes. If you have enough room in your cooler, make your batter the evening before, cover it with cellophane and let it sit in the cooler overnight. This gives the yeast time to work and your pancakes will be lighter and fluffier than ever.

Also, if you like your coffee you will want to get a small percolator. The stove will provide more than enough heat to give you a great cup of coffee in the morning.

Lunch

A camping lunch is almost always on the go. Pack a light lunch with simple things like fruit, sandwiches, and nuts.

Dinner

Dinner is maybe the most important meal of any camping excursion. This is where you will be using those roasting sticks and pie makers.

Hotdogs for dinner, marshmallows for dessert, who could ask for more? Well, your kids will if this is all you plan on brining. So, what else should you bring along?

You can use the stove for simple recipes like hamburgers, brats or even stir fry if you bring along a bag of frozen vegetables. The only real limit is how much cookware you feel like bringing along or cleaning on a given evening.

Now, let's say you don't feel like cleaning up or spending a lot of time preparing something, you can break out those pie irons we talked about earlier. Nearly every recipe begins with two slices of bread buttered heavily on the iron-facing side.

From there, you can make a number of different things. The key here is to make sure any meat you use is precooked. You can either cook it on site using your stove or do it at home and then keep it frozen in your cooler.

With that out of the way, here are some ideas for filling those pie irons:

- **Grilled cheese** (include ham or turkey)

- **Hamburger**

- **BBQ**

- **Sloppy Joes** (hamburger, sauce, seasoning)

- **Pizza** (add pepperoni, cheese and sauce)

- **Pie** (add apple, cherry or pie filling)

Snacks

If you are spending a lot of time swimming or hiking on the trail, you and the children are sure to get hungry. Keep the snacks simple and high energy to keep everyone going until the next meal.

- **Granola bars**

- **Vegetables** (carrots, peppers, celery)

- **Fruit** (apples, bananas, oranges)

- **Trail mix** – Buy premade or save some money and make your own with peanuts, almonds, cashews, dried fruit and chocolate chips for a little extra kick

- **Water** – Naturally, you'll want to stay hydrated. Make sure everyone has a water bottle that you can refill at the campsite.

There is one final recipe to mention before we leave the food aside and go on to what to do when the unexpected happens. That would be the s'more. If for some reason you have not ever had a s'more, then you are truly missing out.

The recipe is simple.

Get a Hershey's chocolate bar, roast a marshmallow and sandwich them between a graham cracker. The result is a dessert that the children will be sure to remember.

Use these ideas (and feel free to add your own) and your family will be sure to be fed and happy for the entire length of your camping trip.

Chapter 4 – When Plan A Fails

No matter how well-planned your trip is, you are bound to hit a few bumps along the way.

Now, we are not going to be going over every kind of physical injury that you might encounter along the way. There are a few things to keep in mind though.

- **First aid** – Get a kit with a basic treatment guide. Also make sure it includes different sizes of Band-Aids, bandages, gauze, hospital tape, aspirin, and alcohol pads.

- **CPR** – If no one in the family is certified in CPR, you should at least get a guide on how to do it. Preferably, have at least one family member certified through a job or community sponsored program before the trip.

- **Cold packs** – These are small packs containing different chemicals that when they interact will generate a cold reaction. Keep a couple of these in your backpack to deal with sprains or other bumps and bruises on the trail.

At least as likely as a physical injury is that most dreaded bane of campers – rain. Unexpected rain will kill a camping trip faster than hoard of the most aggressive mosquitoes you can imagine.

The best thing you can do is make sure that you have a good back up plan.

There are other reasons to have a backup plan. The kids may be tired of trails and even swimming every day and start complaining. The beach may be rocky, trails or other planned attractions may be closed off.

There are any number of reasons to have a Plan B (and C and D if necessary). Here are a handful of options to consider:

- **Playing cards** – This actually belongs in the essentials category. Having a deck of cards when camping is indispensable for rainy days or evenings when some of the family has turned in early and the rest need a quiet activity.

  Teach the kids Go Fish, Old Maid, Hearts, Spades or any other game that comes to mind.

  If you don't already know any, look up the rules on your smartphone.

- **Board games** – Pick something that can be done in a few minutes like Connect Four. Stay away from long games with a lot of small pieces like Monopoly.

- **Plan a movie day** – Especially if this is the first camping trip, around half-way through, people may be starting to get anxious for their creature comforts.

  To prevent this being a problem, plan a trip into a nearby town for a movie about halfway through the vacation. And know where the closest theater is in case you get a rainy day or two, even if you are only on the second day of the trip.

- **Go out to eat** – Again, this breaks up the routine a bit and also gives the parents a break from cooking and cleaning up.

- **Find local attractions** – As previously mentioned, these can include local history museums, curiosities, zoos or even a theme park. Anything to occupy everyone during a day when the weather just isn't cooperating.

- **Plan a shopping trip** – Nearly everyone likes buying things. If the day is cold and rainy, head to the nearest town to spend some time looking for souvenirs to remember the trip. With any luck, they'll help the kids forget all about the bad weather.

- **Tablet** – As a last resort, pack a fully charged tablet or other electronic device.

You can load a handful of movies for an emergency or make sure enough games are installed to keep the children busy when you are making breakfast.

Conclusion

So, you have decided you want to go camping. After you have gone through this guide, you may be thinking that it might be more than you can handle right now.

There are many things to think about and plan for and the task may well seem daunting. But it is not as difficult as it may seem.

Once you get out into the outdoors and experience nature with your family maybe for the first time, it will all be worth it.

Just follow these simple guidelines and you will have a successful camping trip that the family will want to repeat many times in the future.

Online Resources

Where to Camp

Camping Canada

http://www.camping-canada.com/

Top 25 Campsites

http://www.explore-mag.com/the-top-25-campsites-in-canada

What to Bring

Rent-A-Tent Canada

http://www.rent-a-tent-canada.com/

Candadian Adventure Rentals

http://www.canadian-adventure-rentals.com/

REI

https://www.rei.com

Lower Gear

http://www.lowergear.com

Printed in Great Britain
by Amazon

82152140R00020